ZEBULON PIKE

Soldier-Explorer of the American Southwest

CHARLES W.
MAYNARD

The Rosen Publishing Group's
PowerKids Press™
New York

For Janice, my friend and wife

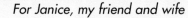

"These vast plains of the western hemisphere, may become in time equally celebrated as the sandy deserts of Africa." Lt. Zebulon Pike

Published in 2003 by The Rosen Publishing Group, Inc.
29 East 21st Street, New York, NY 10010

Copyright © 2003 by The Rosen Publishing Group, Inc.

First Edition

Managing Editor: Kathy Campbell
Book Designer: Maria E. Melendez
Book Layout: Eric DePalo

Photo Credits: Cover and title page, p. 8 (inset), 9 © Independence National Historical Park/National Park Service; p. 4 © Ohio Historical Society; p. 7 (lower left) © Hulton/Archive/Getty Images; pp. 7, 8, 11, 12, 20 © Old Military and Civic Records; p. 11 (inset) © Hulton-Deutsch Collection/CORBIS; p. 12 (bottom) © Denver Public Library; p. 13 © The Smithsonian Institution; p. 15 © Bettmann/CORBIS; p. 16 © Library of Congress; p. 19 (inset) © Library of Congress; p. 19 Maria Melendez.

Maynard, Charles W. (Charles William), 1955–
Zebulon Pike : soldier explorer of the American Southwest / Charles W. Maynard.
  p. cm. — (Famous explorers of the American West)
Includes bibliographical references and index.
Summary: Chronicles Zebulon Pike's exploration of territories within the Louisiana Purchase early in the nineteenth century, including his discovery of what is now known as Pike's Peak.
  ISBN 0-8239-6286-5
1. Pike, Zebulon Montgomery, 1779–1813—Juvenile literature. 2. Explorers—West (U.S.)—Biography—Juvenile literature. 3. West (U.S.)—Discovery and exploration—Juvenile literature. 4. Southwest, New—Discovery and exploration—Juvenile literature. 5. Pikes Peak (Colo.)—Discovery and exploration—Juvenile literature. 6. West (U.S.)—Biography—Juvenile literature. [1. Pike, Zebulon Montgomery, 1779–1813. 2. Explorers. 3. Southwest, New—Discovery and exploration. 4. West (U.S.)—Discovery and exploration.] I. Title. II. Series.
  F592.P653 M39 2003
  917.704'2'092—dc21

2001004880

Manufactured in the United States of America

CONTENTS

Fort Washington was located on the western frontier, near today's Cincinnati, Ohio. In 1793, when young Pike lived at the fort, the frontier stretched from Lake Michigan to today's Georgia.

ebulon Pike was born on January 5, 1779, to Zebulon and Isabella Brown Pike in Lamberton (today's Trenton), New Jersey. Young Zebulon did not get his middle name, Montgomery, for several years. Zebulon's father served in the Continental army during the **American Revolution**. His parents gave Zebulon his middle name in honor of the Revolutionary War hero Richard Montgomery.

When Zebulon was 14 years old, his father became the commander of Fort Washington, near the Ohio River. Fort Washington was one of the many **outposts** built near the edge of America's western frontier. When he was 15 years old, Zebulon joined the Army. As a soldier, during his travels along the Ohio River, he met Clarissa Brown. He and Clarissa married in 1801.

UP THE MISSISSIPPI RIVER

In 1803, President Thomas Jefferson purchased the Louisiana **Territory** from France. The United States needed to know about its new territory. In 1805, the **governor** of Upper Louisiana, General James Wilkinson, asked **Lieutenant** Zebulon Pike to explore the Mississippi River and find its source. He also asked Pike to take notes about the Native Americans who lived along the river and to make peace treaties with them.

Pike left St. Louis with 20 men on August 9, 1805, in a **keelboat** (see map on page 19). After journeying 400 miles (644 km) up the Mississippi, his **expedition** reached Prairie du Chien, in today's Wisconsin. On September 23, on an island now called Pike Island, Minnesota, he signed a treaty with the **Sioux council** to buy land for a fort.

Top: *Pike drew this map of the Mississippi River and wrote a note about the Falls of Saint Anthony.* Bottom: *A nineteenth-century illustration shows the falls, which are in today's Minneapolis, Minnesota.*

Top: *Pike drew this map of the Mississippi and Crow Wing Rivers in late October 1805. Bottom: Charles Willson Peale painted this picture of Zebulon Montgomery Pike in 1808.*

THE SEARCH FOR THE SOURCE

Pike and his men journeyed northward. In October 1805, as winter began, they built a **stockade** near the Swan River. They hunted game and traded with the Native Americans for wild rice. In December, using some sleds, Pike and the men moved on, hoping to find the source of the Mississippi. On January 8, 1806, they reached Sandy Lake, and on February 1 they came to Leech Lake. Pike believed that Leech Lake was the source of the Mississippi River. Today we know that the actual source is Lake Itasca. Pike and his men were freezing and hungry, so they spent little time exploring the area. Pike claimed the area for the United States.

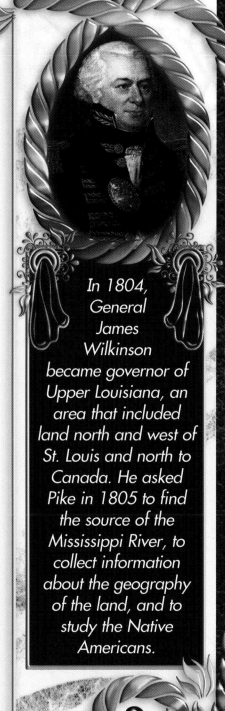

In 1804, General James Wilkinson became governor of Upper Louisiana, an area that included land north and west of St. Louis and north to Canada. He asked Pike in 1805 to find the source of the Mississippi River, to collect information about the geography of the land, and to study the Native Americans.

9

Soon after Pike returned to St. Louis on April 30, 1806, General Wilkinson asked him to **escort** 59 Osage men, women, and children to their village on the Osage River. These people had been captured by the Potawatomi. Americans had freed the Osage and wanted to send them back home. Pike's journey would take him near the Spanish territory of Mexico. The general also asked Pike to seek the sources of the Red and Arkansas Rivers.

The general's son, James B. Wilkinson, joined the expedition to the Southwest. On July 15, 1806, Pike's group left to go up the Missouri and Osage Rivers (see map on page 19). The Osage and the hunters for the group walked along the riverbanks. Pike kept a journal and drew maps to help people learn about the Great Plains.

Top: *Three Osage warriors are pictured in a drawing from the early 1900s.* Bottom: *Pike made notes and maps about the Grand Osage and the Little Osage villages along the Osage River.*

Top: *In his journal, Pike wrote about the Pawnee war party his expedition met on the Great Plains.* Bottom: *A photograph from the late 1800s shows a Pawnee man and woman in front of tepees.*

THE STARS AND STRIPES FLIES OVER THE PLAINS

Zebulon Pike's group reached the Osage village on August 15, 1806. The villagers warmly welcomed their family and friends who had been away for so long. After a visit, Pike's group crossed today's Kansas to reach the Republican River. A Pawnee village stood on the river's banks. A Spanish flag fluttered over the chief's lodge. A Spanish **cavalry** troop had given it to the chief only a month earlier. Pike told the Pawnee that the United States claimed the territory. He said the Pawnee could not be loyal to two countries. After a while, an old Pawnee man lowered the Spanish flag and raised the U.S. flag that Pike had given him.

Pike gave the Pawnee a U.S. flag to raise instead of the Spanish one they flew. In 1806, the U.S. flag had 15 stars and stripes, which represented the first 13 states plus Vermont and Kentucky. In 1818, the flag changed to one star for each state and one stripe for each of the 13 original states.

13

PIKES PEAK

On October 28, 1806, Pike sent Wilkinson and five men down the Arkansas until it met the Mississippi River. The rest of the group, including Pike, turned southwest to find the Arkansas River's source. Pike's group entered today's Colorado. Soon they saw the Rocky Mountains in the distance. Snow began to fall while they were still on the Great Plains. On November 15, they spotted the snow-covered "Mexican Mountains." In his journal, Pike wrote that the mountains looked like "a small blue cloud." It took nine days for Pike to reach the base of the high peaks. Pike took a few men to try to climb the highest mountain. The "Grand Peak" was later named Pikes Peak. Although they tried to find a good route to the top of the peak, they could not. They were tired, cold, and hungry.

They had to turn back because of the deep snow and the lack of food. The weather was so cold that Pike's ink froze. He wrote in his journal with a pencil made from a lead bullet. He and his men moved south to search for the Red River's source. In January 1807, they built a stockade for shelter. The outlook was bleak.

Snow-covered Pikes Peak, near today's Colorado Springs, Colorado, looked like "a small blue cloud" on November 15, 1806, according to Pike. He tried to climb to the top of the peak but could not.

The Spaniards took Pike to Santa Fe's Palace of the Governors. Santa Fe's governor, Joaquin del Real Alencaster, lived here. When he met Pike to ask about the expedition, he thought Pike was a spy.

PRISONERS OF THE SPANIARDS

Lieutenant Pike did not know he was in Spanish territory. He was not on the Red River, but on the Rio Grande. At the end of February 1807, Spanish soldiers arrived to tell Pike that he was in Spanish territory. The Spaniards escorted Pike and his men to Santa Fe in New Spain to meet Santa Fe's governor. The governor seized Pike's journals, because he thought Pike was a spy. The Spaniards took Pike to Chihuahua on **El Camino Real**, or the Royal Road, for more questioning. El Camino Real linked Santa Fe with El Paso, Chihuahua, and Mexico City. Pike began a new journal on scraps of paper he hid in the barrels of his men's rifles. He wrote about the villages he passed and the people he saw. In Chihuahua, Spanish commander Antonio Salcedo met Pike to ask about his trip.

Lieutenant Pike was kept in Chihuahua, Mexico, for about a month. He asked that he and his men be returned to the United States. Commander Salcedo agreed to let them leave. Pike and his men rode back on El Camino Real and the Old San Antonio Road with a Spanish escort. Pike recorded all that he saw while traveling in Mexico and Texas, which was also a Spanish territory. They passed through villages that were more than 200 years old. One of these was San Antonio de Bexar (today's San Antonio, Texas). Pike arrived in Natchitoches, Louisiana, on July 1, 1807, nearly a year after he had left St. Louis. Pike's family came from St. Louis to meet him. They then went with him to Washington, D.C., where Pike gave a report about his explorations to the U.S. government.

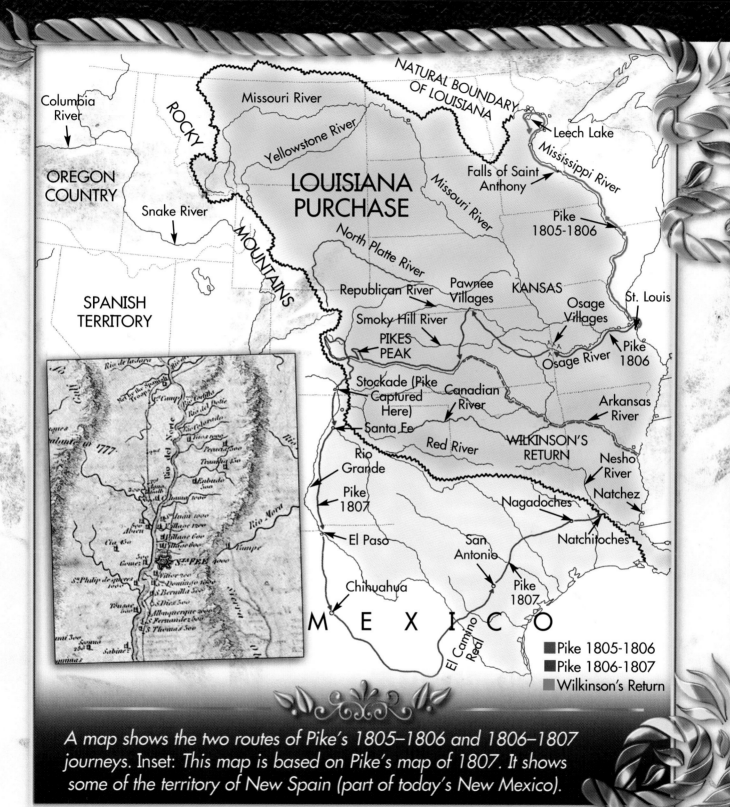

Columbia River

ROCKY

OREGON COUNTRY

Snake River

MOUNTAINS

SPANISH TERRITORY

Missouri River

Yellowstone River

NATURAL BOUNDARY OF LOUISIANA

Leech Lake

Mississippi River

Falls of Saint Anthony

LOUISIANA PURCHASE

Missouri River

Pike 1805-1806

North Platte River

Republican River

Pawnee Villages

KANSAS

St. Louis

Smoky Hill River

Osage Villages

PIKES PEAK

Osage River

Pike 1806

Stockade (Pike Captured Here)

Canadian River

Arkansas River

Santa Fe

Red River

WILKINSON'S RETURN

Nesho River

Rio Grande

Pike 1807

Natchez

Nagadoches

Natchitoches

El Paso

San Antonio

Pike 1807

Chihuahua

M E X I C O

El Camino Real

■ Pike 1805-1806
■ Pike 1806-1807
■ Wilkinson's Return

*A map shows the two routes of Pike's 1805–1806 and 1806–1807
journeys. Inset: This map is based on Pike's map of 1807. It shows
some of the territory of New Spain (part of today's New Mexico).*

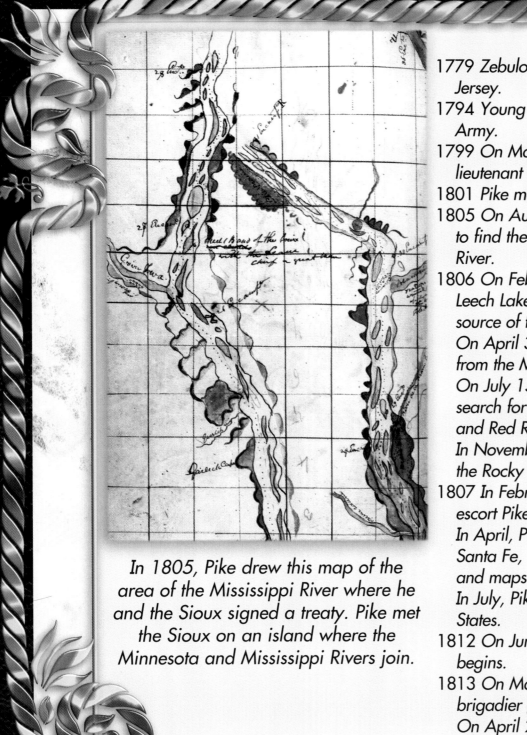

In 1805, Pike drew this map of the area of the Mississippi River where he and the Sioux signed a treaty. Pike met the Sioux on an island where the Minnesota and Mississippi Rivers join.

TIMELINE

1779 Zebulon Pike is born in New Jersey.

1794 Young Zebulon joins the U.S. Army.

1799 On March 3, Pike becomes a lieutenant in the U.S. Army.

1801 Pike marries Clarissa Brown.

1805 On August 9, Pike leaves St. Louis to find the source of the Mississippi River.

1806 On February 1, Pike reaches Leech Lake, which he believes is the source of the Mississippi River.
On April 30, he returns to St. Louis from the Mississippi expedition.
On July 15, he leaves St. Louis to search for the sources of the Arkansas and Red Rivers.
In November, Pike and his men see the Rocky Mountains and Pikes Peak.

1807 In February, Spanish soldiers escort Pike to Santa Fe.
In April, Pike visits the governor in Santa Fe, who takes away his journal and maps.
In July, Pike returns to the United States.

1812 On June 18, the War of 1812 begins.

1813 On March 12, Pike becomes a brigadier general in the U.S. Army.
On April 27, Pike dies after being injured in the Battle of York.

Pike loved to read books wherever he went. He even carried books and paper on his expeditions up the Mississippi and into the Rocky Mountains. His journals were very valuable in telling Americans what the western territory of the United States looked like in the early 1800s. He took notes about the land. He wrote about Native American people, their customs, and their cultures. Pike clearly described the Spanish villages he passed through in New Mexico, Mexico, and Texas.

While in Washington, D.C., Pike worked on his journals, and in 1810, he **published** them. The journal that the Spanish governor had taken stayed in Mexico until 1908, when it was returned to the United States. Today it is protected in the National Archives in Washington, D.C.

PIKE'S LEGACY

On March 12, 1813, Zebulon Pike was made a **brigadier general**. At the time, the United States was fighting Great Britain in the War of 1812. This war was about the freedom of ships to sail on the oceans. It was also being fought over America's settlement in the western territories. During the war, Pike and his troops attacked York (today's Toronto), in Canada. As the British fled, they blew up their **powder magazine**, which wounded Pike. He died on April 27, 1813.

Today the memory of Pike lives on in the names of many places. The most famous of these places is Pikes Peak. After Katharine Lee Bates traveled to the top of Pikes Peak in 1893, she wrote the poem "America the Beautiful," which became a popular song about the United States.

GLOSSARY

American Revolution (uh-MER-uh-ken reh-vuh-LOO-shun) A war that colonists in America fought from 1775 to 1783 to win freedom from England.

brigadier general (brih-guh-DEER JEN-rul) A high-ranking army officer.

cavalry (KA-vul-ree) The part of the army that rides horses.

council (KOWN-sul) A group called together to give advice and to discuss or to settle questions.

El Camino Real (EL kuh-MEE-no ray-AHL) Spanish for "the Royal Road" or "King's Highway." El Camino Real was a major trade route between Santa Fe and Mexico City.

escort (es-KORT) To go along with others to lead them to a specific place.

expedition (ek-spuh-DIH-shun) A journey for a special purpose, such as scientific study.

governor (GUH-vuh-nur) An official who is elected or is appointed as the head of a state or a territory.

keelboat (KEEL-boht) A large, flat-bottomed boat with a long piece of wood running from the front to the back under the boat. The boat can be rowed, sailed, poled, or pulled by ropes.

lieutenant (loo-TEH-nent) An army officer.

outposts (OWT-pohsts) Settlements that are far away from other places.

powder magazine (POW-dur MA-guh-zeen) A special room for storing gunpowder and explosives.

published (PUH-blishd) To have printed something, such as a book, a story, or a poem, so people can read it.

Sioux (SOO) Native Americans from the North American plains.

stockade (stah-KAYD) A wooden wall made of large, strong posts.

territory (TEHR-uh-tohr-ee) Land that is controlled by a person or a group of people.

INDEX

PRIMARY SOURCES

Pages 7 (top), 8 (top), 11 (bottom), 12 (top), and 20.
Maps and notes from the 1806–1807 journal of Zebulon Montgomery Pike. National Archives, Washington, D.C.
Page 8 (inset). *Zebulon Montgomery Pike.* This is a portrait that was painted in oils in about 1808 by Charles Willson Peale. It is now in Philadelphia's Independence National Historical Park, National Park Service.
Page 9. *James Wilkinson.* Charles Willson Peale painted this portrait around 1797.
Page 12 (bottom). *Pawnee in Nebraska.* This

photograph was taken between 1880 and 1900.
Page 13. *Stars and Stripes.* This U.S. flag flew over Fort McHenry during the Battle of Baltimore in 1814. It inspired Francis Scott Key to write the poem that later became the U.S. anthem, "The Star-Spangled Banner."
Page 19. *Detail of a map of the Internal Provinces of New Spain.* The complete map from which this detail is taken was based on maps actually created by Pike in 1807. The detail shows the region around Santa Fe.

WEB SITES

To learn more about Zebulon Pike, check out these Web sites:
http://dlwgraphics.com/mnpike2.htm
www.kcmuseum.com/explor05.html
www.tsha.utexas.edu/handbook/online/articles/view/PP/fpi19.html